SEIJI OZAWA
Symphony Conductor

"My job is to make a situation where the musicians can have fun and pleasure in making music."

SEIJI OZAWA
Symphony Conductor

By Charnan Simon

CHILDRENS PRESS ®
CHICAGO

PHOTO CREDITS

Steve J. Sherman: cover
Courtesy of Boston Symphony Orchestra: 1, 5, 22, 27
    (right); © Whitestone, 9, 10, 14, 16; © Walter H.
    Scott, 2, 13; © Kinoshita, 27 (left), 31; © Peter Schaaf,
    30; © Christian Steiner, 3, 11, 21, 32
AP/Wide World: 7, 17, 19, 20, 22, 25, 29
Stock Boston: 8
UPI/Bettman: 12, 15
Magnum Photos: © Costa Manos, 23, 24 (two photos);
    © Martine Franck, 26
Ira Wyman, 28

EDITORIAL STAFF

Project Editor: E. Russell Primm III
Design and Electronic Composition: Biner Design
Photo Research: Carol Parden
Editorial Assistance: Ann Duvall

ACKNOWLEDGEMENTS

The editors which to thank Maestro Ozawa, Evans
Mirageas, Artistic Administrator of the Boston
Symphony Orchestra, and the staff at the BSO for
their assistance in the creation of this biography.

To my Father and Mother, from whom I inherited
both my tin ear and my love for music.

Library of Congress Cataloging-in-Publication Data
Simon, Charnan.
    Seiji Ozawa : symphony conductor / by Charnan
Simon.
        p. cm. — (Picture-story biography)
        Summary: A career biography of the Japanese
conductor famous for directing major western orchestras
worldwide.
        ISBN 0-516-04182-7
        1. Ozawa, Seiji, 1935– —Juvenile literature.
2. Conductors (Music)—Biography—Juvenile literature.
[1. Ozawa, Seiji, 1935– . 2. Conductors (Music)] I. Title.
II. Series.
ML3930.095S5 1992   91-36741
784.2'092—dc20   CIP
[B]   AC MN

THE ORCHESTRA hall in Besançon, France, was hushed and still. In the audience, the judges for the 1959 International Competition of Orchestra Conductors waited quietly. Onstage, the musicians got their instruments ready.

Now all eyes were on the young conductor as he took his place at the podium. Seiji Ozawa knew that some people did not think he belonged on

A young Seiji conducts an orchestra rehearsal.

this stage. He was Japanese — an outsider in the tightly knit Western music world. All the great orchestral scores were written by Europeans. How could a Japanese musician conduct such music? Everyone knew it took a European to bring out the best in Western music!

Everyone but Seiji Ozawa, maybe. Confident and calm, he lifted his baton to begin the concert. By the time he put it down again at music's end, the audience understood what Seiji had known all along. Seiji Ozawa, the 24-year-old "outsider," had won first prize.

Seiji Ozawa was born on September 1, 1935, in Shenyang, China. His parents were Japanese, and toward the end of World War II in 1944, the family moved back to Japan.

Seiji and his three brothers studied music from an early age. That in itself

Seiji and his mother, Sakura, during the Boston Symphony Orchestra's tour through China in 1979

was not so unusual. What was
unusual was that the four Ozawa boys
studied European and American music
as well as Japanese music. Seiji took
piano lessons. One of his older
brothers studied the cello. At home,
the family listened to American and
European records, sang black

Japanese Americans perform Japanese music on traditional instruments.

spirituals, and took turns playing the accordion. These instruments, and this kind of music, were very different from the instruments and music of Japan.

Seiji's mother and father recognized their son's musical talent. They encouraged him in all he did. Soon Seiji was a student at the famed Toho Gakuen School of Music in Tokyo. Here he decided that, much as he liked playing music, he liked conducting music more. He especially liked conducting orchestral music! An orchestra is made up of many musicians, playing many different kinds of instruments. The person who leads the orchestra and helps the musicians perform their best is called the conductor. Seiji Ozawa liked being a conductor — and he was good at it, too. He was so good, he won first prize in conducting when he graduated from the Toho Gakuen School.

Seiji, early in his career, conducts a concert at the Tanglewood Festival.

Seiji's favorite teacher in Tokyo was a man named Hideo Saito. As a young man, Saito had studied in Germany with the great European musicans of the time. Saito knew that Japan could not offer Seiji all the training he needed. Orchestral music has it roots in Europe. If Seiji was serious about becoming an orchestra conductor, he, too, must travel to Europe.

Learning to conduct an orchestra is complex and difficult. Here, the instructor on the right watches as Seiji works with the orchestra.

Conducting a full orchestra requires deep concentration on the part of the conductor.

And so, in 1959, Seiji said good-bye to Japan and sailed to Europe. He was prepared to work hard and learn much. What he was not prepared for was the Europeans' reactions to his ambitions. For many Europeans, it was unthinkable that a Japanese should want to conduct classic Western music. It just wasn't traditional! "I realized that what I was doing was strange only when I got to Europe," remembers Seiji.

Seiji may have been surprised by Western reaction, but he was not discouraged. Within a year he had won first prize at the International Competition of Orchestra Conductors in Besançon. Seiji Ozawa had proven himself a force to be reckoned with!

One of the judges in Besançon was a man named Charles Munch. Munch was the music director of the Boston

Charles Munch was an important influence on the young Seiji. Below, Charles Munch (right) chats with his successor at the Boston Symphony Orchestra, Erich Leinsdorf.

The Boston Symphony Orchestra moves to the Bershire Mountains in western Massachussets every summer. The Tanglewood Festival presents some of the finest summer concerts in North America.

Symphony Orchestra. "I simply loved him," Ozawa says, looking back. "I went to him and asked, 'Would you teach me?' " Munch was equally impressed with the young Japanese conductor. He invited Seiji to come to Tanglewood, Massachusetts, the following summer. Tanglewood is the summer home of the Boston Symphony Orchestra. It is also the site of the Berkshire Music Center, the

BSO's summer school for advanced musicians. It was to the Berkshire Music Center that Seiji Ozawa came as a student conductor.

When Seiji arrived at Tanglewood, he spoke very little English. That might have been a problem for some people, but not for Seiji. Letting the music be his guide, he communicated his feelings and his musical ideas through his body. The technique worked. At the end of the summer, he was awarded the Koussevitzky Prize for outstanding student conductor.

Mme. Koussevitzky presents Seiji with the Koussevitzky Prize for outstanding student conductor. The prize was named for her late husband Serge Koussevitzky, the famed conductor of the Boston Symphony Orchestra.

Herbert von Karjan

From Tanglewood, Seiji headed back across the Atlantic to Europe. His goal this time was to study with the famous Herbert von Karjan. Von Karjan was the conductor of the Berlin Philharmonic Orchestra. Studying with him was the dream of every young conductor. When Seiji won a scholarship from the city of Berlin to do just that, the European music world took notice.

Seiji was noticed on the other side of the Atlantic, too. The conductor of the New York Philharmonic was a man named Leonard Bernstein. Mr. Bernstein liked what he had seen and heard of von Karjan's talented student. He invited Seiji Ozawa to become an assistant conductor of the New York Philharmonic for the 1961–1962 season.

At age 27, Seiji Ozawa was showing Europe and America that a Japanese

Leonard Bernstein (left), the conductor of the New York Philharmonic, is shown here with Seiji. Bernstein was one of Seiji's earliest and strongest supporters.

Seiji has conducted most of the world's greatest orchestras. In November 1962, he conducted the Detroit Symphony.

could, indeed, become one of the world's finest conductors of orchestral music. Now it was time to show Japan how well its native son had done.

And so, in December 1962, Seiji Ozawa returned to Japan to conduct a series of concerts with Japan's most famous orchestra, the NHK Symphony.

It should have been a triumphant homecoming. But not all Japanese musicians liked Seiji. Many of them thought he was just a cocky youngster. They might appreciate his talents, but they didn't think he showed the proper respect. It offended their Japanese dignity to see him "showing off" his youth and abilities. In Japan, fitting in was more important than standing out. And with all his talents, Seiji Ozawa couldn't help but stand out.

So when Seiji Ozawa raised his baton that December day in 1962, he stood alone on the stage. The Japanese musicians simply refused to play for him. By walking out, they reminded Seiji that Eastern ways were different from Western ways. As the Japanese proverb says: "The nail that sticks out is hammered down."

It was a hard lesson for Seiji Ozawa. In the West, his great talents were applauded. In his homeland of Japan,

The Toronto Symphony was one of the several orchestras with which Seiji has been associated.

they were respected — but they were also resented. Seiji Ozawa might be admired as a role model for thousands of young Japanese who wanted to learn classical Western music. But he was also scorned as a musician who was not purely Japanese. All his life, Seiji would fight to be both things — a strong Japanese and a strong conductor of Western music.

Seiji went back to North America after his Japanese tour in 1962. His career blossomed. He was named music director of the Chicago Symphony Orchestra's Ravinia Festival for five summers, from 1964 to 1968. During the winters of those years, he was the music director of the Toronto Symphony Orchestra in Canada.

After Toronto, Seiji traveled west to San Francisco. He served as music director of the San Francisco Symphony

In 1973, the San Francisco Symphony and Maestro Ozawa traveled to Leningrad to perform a series of concerts.

This formal portrait of the Boston Symphony Orchestra was taken in Boston's Symphony Hall in 1988.

from 1970 to 1976, and was later named the orchestra's music advisor.

Ever since Charles Munch had invited him to Tanglewood in 1959, Seiji had had a special relationship with the Boston Symphony. This relationship was cemented in 1973, when Seiji Ozawa was named music director of the Boston Symphony Orchestra. He has held this position ever since.

Seiji Ozawa's years with the Boston Symphony have been busy and exciting. He and the orchestra have toured all over North America and the world. In Europe, they've visited France, Germany, Austria, England, Greece, the Netherlands, and Belgium.

Seiji and the Boston Symphony haven't just visited Western capitals. They have traveled to Japan four times

In February 1986, Seiji introduced his orchestra members to Japan's Crown Prince Akihito, left, and Crown Princess Michiko in Tokyo. Below, Seiji joins BSO members in a baseball game during their tour of Japan.

*During the BSO's tour in China, Seiji led classes for young
Chinese conductors.*

and to Hong Kong once. And in March
1979 they made an historic visit to
China.

The China trip was exciting for
many reasons. For seven straight days,
the American and Chinese musicians
attended classes, held practice sessions,
and tried out each other's instruments.
Mostly, they shared their love of music.

*Left, Seiji listens as Chinese pianists perform.
Above , Seiji greets a crowd of admiring
classical music fans.*

"It was incredible," remembers Seiji,
"how much the musicians had to
communicate. They talked even more
than they played. We kept the
interpreters very busy!" The tour
climaxed when the Boston Symphony
joined with the Central Philharmonic
Orchestra of Beijing to play Beethoven's
Fifth Symphony. The audience of 18,000
went wild — especially when the joint

orchestra played an encore of "The Stars and Stripes Forever." It was a thrilling musical meeting of East and West!

Besides conducting the Boston Symphony, Seiji Ozawa travels all over the world as a guest conductor for other major orchestras. He also spends a lot of time making recordings of his favorite musical pieces. And no matter how busy he is, he always makes time to teach conducting students at the Berkshire Music Center each summer.

Arthur Fiedler, the conductor for the Boston Pops orchestra, greets Seiji as he returns from China.

Opera is a great passion of Seiji's. Here, he conducts an orchestra during a dress rehearsal.

One of Seiji Ozawa's favorite kinds of music is opera. In opera, singers act out a dramatic story while the orchestra accompanies them on their instruments. The conductor of an opera has to pay attention to the singers, the orchestra, and the elaborate stage settings and props. It is a huge undertaking — but Seiji Ozawa loves it.

Today, Seiji Ozawa is one of the Western world's great classical conductors. His public life is very busy and takes him all over the world. Still, in private, Seiji is very much Japanese. He and his wife Vera have chosen to raise their son and daughter in Japan, in the same neighborhood Seiji himself grew up in.

Seiji tries to see his family once a month, and he talks to them on the

Left, Seiji and his wife Vera arrive in Nagasaki, Japan. Right, Seiji holds one of his children.

*Three of the 20th century's greatest classical music figures
gather to celebrate the 40th anniversary of the Berkshire Music
Center: Aaron Copeland (left), Leonard Bernstein (center), and
Seiji Ozawa (right).*

telephone every day. But the best time
of year is summer, when the whole
family lives together in Tanglewood.
For three months, Seiji shares his time
with his family, the musicians at
Tanglewood, and the students at the
Berkshire Music Center.

There are still some critics who
question whether Seiji Ozawa, a
Japanese, can truly play and conduct
Western music. Seiji himself does not

pay much attention to such critics. "Western music is so organized," he once said. "It is so strong and so logical that it is very easy for every nationality to learn."

Still, Seiji knows how hard it can be to combine his Japanese heritage with his Western profession. As he watches other young Asian performers rise in the musical world, he knows they, too, will have a hard time combining the two cultures.

Seiji with the young violinist Midori at Carnegie Hall, February 1991

In a documentary film of his life made in 1984, Seiji Ozawa questioned his musical and professional choices. "Sometimes I say, 'Why did I become a Western music musician?' I think that made my life much more interesting, and much more exciting. Of course, I have to pay a price."

Whatever the price paid for a life of hard choices, the rest of the world has much to thank Seiji Ozawa for. He has coaxed beautiful music out of

Rudolf Serkin performs a piano concerto as Seiji conducts the orchestra.

orchestras around the world. He has opened the door for other Asian musicians wishing to enter the Western music world. And he has shown that, whatever our cultural differences, music can, indeed, be the great communicator.

"Western music is like the sun," Seiji Ozawa says. "All over the world, the sunset is different, but the beauty is the same. Maybe there is a way to make a marriage between this Oriental blood and Western music."

Seiji Ozawa

1935	September 1 — Born in Shenyang, China
1944	Moved with family back to Japan
1958	Graduated from the Toho Gakuen School of Music in Tokyo with first prizes in conducting and composing
1959	Won first prize at the International Competition of Orchestra Conductors in Besançon, France
1960	Awarded the Berkshire Music Center's highest honor, the Koussevitzky Prize for student conductor
1960–61	Scholarship study with Herbert von Karjan of the Berlin Philharmonic Orchestra
1961–62	Named assistant conductor of the New York Philharmonic Orchestra
1964–68	Music director of the Chicago Symphony Orchestra's Ravinia Festival
1965–69	Music director of the Toronto Symphony Orchestra
1970–76	Music director of the San Francisco Symphony
1970	Named artistic director of the Tanglewood Festival
1973	Music director of the Boston Symphony Orchestra
1975	Won an Emmy for the BSO's "Evening at the Symphony" PBS television series
1975	Awarded an honorary doctor of music degree from the University of Massachusetts
1979	March 13–19 — Took Boston Symphony on historic trip to China
1982	Awarded an honorary doctor of music degree from the New England Conservatory of Music
1984	Awarded an honorary doctor of music degree from Wheaton College

Index

About the Author

Charnan Simon lives with her husband and two daughters in Chicago, Illinois. Her house is a not-too-long train ride away from Orchestra Hall, where she goes to hear the Chicago Symphony Orchestra play gorgeous music every chance she gets. Ms. Simon also likes to write books for young readers. She can't listen and write at the same time, though — she gets so distracted by the music that she forgets to finish her work. If she weren't a writer, Ms. Simon would like to play the bassoon.